BY HIS WORD AND SPIRIT:
APPLYING MY HEART
TO UNDERSTANDING

Copyright

© 2025 Lord & Benoit Publishing

ISBN: 978-0-9888692-9-5

This is a Scripture workbook. Scripture workbooks are Bible passages on a particular subject, followed by questions that inspire Interactive Bible Learning on that subject. The Holy Bible is not copyrighted, but the translations can be.

Each publisher extends gratis permission to use their *translation* of the Bible when less than 500/1000 verses from each translation are quoted. Links to detailed rights for each translator/publisher are below. This book complies with all translation acknowledgement requirements.

Scripture quotations marked (AMPC) were taken from the Amplified® Bible, Copyright © 1954, 1958, 1962, 1964, 1965, 1987 by The Lockman Foundation. Used by permission. All rights reserved. www.lockman.org" https://www.lockman.org/permission-to-quote-copyright-trademark-information/

Scripture quotations marked (NASB1995) were from the New American Standard Bible®, Copyright © 1960, 1971, 1977, 1995 by The Lockman Foundation. Used by permission. All rights reserved. www.lockman.org" https://www.lockman.org/permission-to-quote-copyright-trademark-information/

Scripture marked (NKJV) were from the New King James Version®. Copyright © 1982 by Thomas Nelson. Used by permission. All rights reserved.
https://www.thomasnelson.com/about-us/permissions/#permissionBiblequote

Scripture quotations marked (ESV) are from the ESV® Bible (The Holy Bible, English Standard Version®), copyright © 2001 by Crossway, a publishing ministry of Good News Publishers. Used by permission. All rights reserved."
https://www.crossway.org/permissions/

Scripture marked (WEB) were from the World English Bible. The name "World English Bible" is trademarked. The World English Bible is a no copyright Modern English translation of the Holy Bible. The World English Bible is based on the American Standard Version of the Holy Bible first published in 1901, the Biblia Hebraica Stutgartensa Old Testament, and the Greek Majority Text New Testament. For more information, please see the World English Bible Frequently Asked Questions and the legal and status page at
https://ebible.org/eng-web/copyright.htm

Acknowledgements

Lead Contributor: B Benoit

Prayer Support: L Benoit

Prioritization Contributor(s): A Bese, D Bese

Cover Illustrator: A Bese

Cover Photo: Christian Engagement Picture by Bible verses 70

Inspiration for this Scripture Workbook

The inspiration for this Scripture workbook initially came from my wife, who, during her study time, compiled the three gospel accounts of the parable of the sower of the seed. She observed that the "good ground" represents a person who hears the Word of God, understands it with their heart (and I would add, with the help of the Holy Spirit), and applies it in their life. This is the one who bears fruit—some thirty, sixty, or a hundredfold—with patience and perseverance. The passages in this Scripture workbook center around the theme of "gaining understanding with the heart." True spiritual growth comes not just from hearing the Word but from internalizing it, allowing it to take root, and walking it out in faith.

The questions and leadership approach is Interactive Bible Learning (IBL). The IBL methodology was shaped by years of study and countless focused Bible learning sessions. All things work together to help leaders lead a study that remains focused on Jesus Christ and the Word of God. These meetings should encourage a balance of truth and grace in communication, foster deep interaction where no one remains hidden, and cultivate an atmosphere of dependence on the Holy Spirit (and one another) for understanding. In such an environment, we often witness profound personal growth, as individuals engage in self-discovery of Jesus Christ through His Word.

~ B Benoit

Contents

#1	Proverbs 2:1-11 (WEB)	1
#2	Isaiah 11:1-5 (NKJV)	2
#3	Proverbs 3:1-12 (WEB)	3
#4	Proverbs 3:13-26 (AMPC)	4
#5	Matthew 7:13-8:1 (WEB)	6
#6	Proverbs 4:1-13 (NKJV)	8
#7	Matthew 13:1-9, 18-23 (WEB)	10
#8	Proverbs 5:1-10 (WEB)	12
#9	Proverbs 16:16-25 (WEB)	13
#10	Matthew 13:10-17 (NASB1995)	14
#11	Proverbs 8:1-21 (WEB)	16
#12	Proverbs 9 (WEB)	18
#13	Proverbs 10:15-23 (NASB1995)	20
#14	Proverbs 14:26-35 (NASB1995)	22
#15	Proverbs 17:16-28 (WEB)	24
#16	Proverbs 15:11-22 (WEB)	26
#17	Proverbs 18:10-15 (ESV)	27
#18	Proverbs 19:1-8 (NKJV)	28
#19	Proverbs 22:17-29 (NASB1995)	29
#20	Proverbs 23:12-23 (NKJV)	30
#21	Proverbs 24:1-11 (NKJV)	31
#22	Proverbs 28:1-15 (WEB)	32
For further learning		35
#23	Proverbs 24:12-22 (WEB)	35

#	Reference	Page
#24	Proverbs 28:16-28 (WEB)	36
#25	Ecclesiastes 7:8-14 (NASB1995)	37
#26	Ecclesiastes 7:15-29 (AMPC)	38
#27	Mark 12:28-40 (WEB)	40
#28	Romans 12:1-9 (AMPC)	42
#29	Philippians 4:1-13 (WEB)	44
#30	John 7:14-24 (WEB)	46
#31	Ephesians 5:15-24 (WEB)	47
#32	Proverbs 29:1-15 (WEB)	48
#33	Colossians 3:12-17 (NKJV)	49
#34	Daniel 1:15-21 (WEB)	50
#35	Matthew 11:25-30 (NASB1995)	51
#36	1 Corinthians 1:18-31 (WEB)	52
#37	Ephesians 1:15-2:3 (NKJV)	54
#38	2 Timothy 3 (WEB)	56
#39	James 3 (WEB)	58
#40	Ecclesiastes 10 (AMPC)	60
#41	Colossians 2:1-10 (ESV)	62
#42	Ecclesiastes 1:12-18 (AMPC)	63
#43	1 John 5:10-21 (WEB)	64
#44	Daniel 2:16-23 (WEB)	66
#45	Hosea 14 (WEB)	67
#46	Colossians 1:1-14 (NASB1995)	68
#47	2 Timothy 2:1-14 (WEB)	70
#48	Proverbs 18:1-9 (ESV)	72
#49	Luke 2:45-52 (WEB)	73

Appendix A – Instructor Guide for Interactive Bible Learning 75

Appendix B – The Good News 78

#1 Proverbs 2:1-11 (WEB)

My son, if you will receive my words, and store up my commandments within you, ²so as to turn your ear to wisdom, and apply your heart to understanding; ³yes, if you call out for discernment, and lift up your voice for understanding; ⁴if you seek her as silver, and search for her as for hidden treasures: ⁵then you will understand the fear of Yahweh, and find the knowledge of God. ⁶For Yahweh gives wisdom. Out of his mouth comes knowledge and understanding. ⁷He lays up sound wisdom for the upright. He is a shield to those who walk in integrity, ⁸that he may guard the paths of justice, and preserve the way of his saints. ⁹Then you will understand righteousness and justice, equity and every good path. ¹⁰For wisdom will enter into your heart. Knowledge will be pleasant to your soul. ¹¹Discretion will watch over you. Understanding will keep you,

What insight does God give us about applying our hearts to understand what He is saying in Scripture?

What distractions are noted in this text that might tempt someone to not apply their heart to spiritual understanding?

Take a minute and ask the Lord how He wants you to apply this Scripture to your life going forward (and we'll go around the room)?

#2 Isaiah 11:1-5 (NKJV)

There shall come forth a Rod from the stem of Jesse, and a Branch shall grow out of his roots. ² The Spirit of the Lord shall rest upon Him, the Spirit of wisdom and understanding, the Spirit of counsel and might, the Spirit of knowledge and of the fear of the Lord. ³ His delight *is* in the fear of the Lord, and He shall not judge by the sight of His eyes, nor decide by the hearing of His ears; ⁴ but with righteousness He shall judge the poor, and decide with equity for the meek of the earth; He shall strike the earth with the rod of His mouth, and with the breath of His lips He shall slay the wicked. ⁵ Righteousness shall be the belt of His loins, and faithfulness the belt of His waist.

What insight does God give us about applying our hearts to understand what He is saying in Scripture?

What distractions are noted in this text that might tempt someone to not apply their heart to spiritual understanding?

Take a minute and ask the Lord how He wants you to apply this Scripture to your life going forward (and we'll go around the room)?

#3 Proverbs 3:1-12 (WEB)

My son, don't forget my teaching; but let your heart keep my commandments: ²for they will add to you length of days, years of life, and peace. ³Don't let kindness and truth forsake you. Bind them around your neck. Write them on the tablet of your heart. ⁴So you will find favor, and good understanding in the sight of God and man. ⁵Trust in Yahweh with all your heart, and don't lean on your own understanding. ⁶In all your ways acknowledge him, and he will make your paths straight. ⁷Don't be wise in your own eyes. Fear Yahweh, and depart from evil. ⁸It will be health to your body, and nourishment to your bones. ⁹Honor Yahweh with your substance, with the first fruits of all your increase: ¹⁰so your barns will be filled with plenty, and your vats will overflow with new wine. ¹¹My son, don't despise Yahweh's discipline, neither be weary of his correction; ¹²for whom Yahweh loves, he corrects, even as a father reproves the son in whom he delights.

What insight does God give us about applying our hearts to understand what He is saying in Scripture?

What distractions are noted in this text that might tempt someone to not apply their heart to spiritual understanding?

Take a minute and ask the Lord how He wants you to apply this Scripture to your life going forward (and we'll go around the room)?

#4 Proverbs 3:13-26 (AMPC)

Happy (blessed, fortunate, enviable) is the man who finds skillful *and* godly Wisdom, and the man who gets understanding [drawing it forth from God's Word and life's experiences], [14] For the gaining of it is better than the gaining of silver, and the profit of it better than fine gold. [15] Skillful *and* godly Wisdom is more precious than rubies; and nothing you can wish for is to be compared to her. [16] Length of days is in her right hand, and in her left hand are riches and honor. [17] Her ways are highways of pleasantness, and all her paths are peace. [18] She is a tree of life to those who lay hold on her; and happy (blessed, fortunate, to be envied) is everyone who holds her fast. [19] The Lord by skillful *and* godly Wisdom has founded the earth; by understanding He has established the heavens. [20] By His knowledge the deeps were broken up, and the skies distill the dew. [21] My son, let them not escape from your sight, but keep sound *and* godly Wisdom and discretion, [22] And they will be life to your inner self, and a gracious ornament to your neck (your outer self). [23] Then you will walk in your way securely *and* in confident trust, and you shall not dash your foot *or* stumble. [24] When you lie down, you shall not be afraid; yes, you shall lie down, and your sleep shall be sweet. [25] Be not afraid of sudden terror *and* panic, nor of the stormy blast *or* the storm and ruin of the wicked when it comes [for you will be guiltless], [26] For the Lord shall be your confidence, firm *and* strong, and shall keep your foot from being caught [in a trap or some hidden danger].

What insight does God give us about applying our hearts to understand what He is saying in Scripture?

What distractions are noted in this text that might tempt someone to not apply their heart to spiritual understanding?

Take a minute and ask the Lord how He wants you to apply this Scripture to your life going forward (and we'll go around the room)?

#5 Matthew 7:13-8:1 (WEB)

"Enter in by the narrow gate; for the gate is wide and the way is broad that leads to destruction, and there are many who enter in by it. [14] How the gate is narrow and the way is restricted that leads to life! There are who find it. [15] "Beware of false prophets, who come to you in sheep's clothing, but inwardly are ravening wolves. [16] By their fruits you will know them. Do you gather grapes from thorns or figs from thistles? [17] Even so, every good tree produces good fruit, but the corrupt tree produces evil fruit. [18] A good tree can't produce evil fruit, neither can a corrupt tree produce good fruit. [19] Every tree that doesn't grow good fruit is cut down and thrown into the fire. [20] Therefore by their fruits you will know them. [21] "Not everyone who says to me, 'Lord, Lord,' will enter into the Kingdom of Heaven, but he who does the will of my Father who is in heaven. [22] Many will tell me in that day, 'Lord, Lord, didn't we prophesy in your name, in your name cast out demons, and in your name do many mighty works?' [23] Then I will tell them, 'I never knew you. Depart from me, you who work iniquity.' [24] "Everyone therefore who hears these words of mine and does them, I will liken him to a wise man who built his house on a rock. [25] The rain came down, the floods came, and the winds blew and beat on that house; and it didn't fall, for it was founded on the rock. [26] Everyone who hears these words of mine and doesn't do them will be like a foolish man who built his house on the sand. [27] The rain came down, the floods came, and the winds blew and beat on that house; and it fell—and its fall was great." [28] When Jesus had finished saying these things, the multitudes were astonished at his teaching, [29] for he taught them with authority, and not like the scribes. [8:1] When he came down from the mountain, great multitudes followed him.

What insight does God give us about applying our hearts to understand what He is saying in Scripture?

What distractions are noted in this text that might tempt someone to not apply their heart to spiritual understanding?

Take a minute and ask the Lord how He wants you to apply this Scripture to your life going forward (and we'll go around the room)?

#6 Proverbs 4:1-13 (NKJV)

Hear, *my* children, the instruction of a father, and give attention to know understanding; ²for I give you good doctrine: do not forsake my law. ³When I was my father's son, tender and the only one in the sight of my mother, ⁴he also taught me, and said to me: "Let your heart retain my words; keep my commands, and live. ⁵Get wisdom! Get understanding! Do not forget, nor turn away from the words of my mouth. ⁶Do not forsake her, and she will preserve you; love her, and she will keep you. ⁷Wisdom *is* the principal thing; *therefore* get wisdom. And in all your getting, get understanding. ⁸Exalt her, and she will promote you; she will bring you honor, when you embrace her. ⁹She will place on your head an ornament of grace; a crown of glory she will deliver to you." ¹⁰Hear, my son, and receive my sayings, and the years of your life will be many. ¹¹I have taught you in the way of wisdom; I have led you in right paths. ¹²When you walk, your steps will not be hindered, and when you run, you will not stumble. ¹³Take firm hold of instruction, do not let go; keep her, for she *is* your life.

What insight does God give us about applying our hearts to understand what He is saying in Scripture?

What distractions are noted in this text that might tempt someone to not apply their heart to spiritual understanding?

Take a minute and ask the Lord how He wants you to apply this Scripture to your life going forward (and we'll go around the room)?

#7   Matthew 13:1-9, 18-23 ^(WEB)

On that day Jesus went out of the house and sat by the seaside. ² Great multitudes gathered to him, so that he entered into a boat and sat; and all the multitude stood on the beach. ³ He spoke to them many things in parables, saying, "Behold, a farmer went out to sow. ⁴ As he sowed, some seeds fell by the roadside, and the birds came and devoured them. ⁵ Others fell on rocky ground, where they didn't have much soil, and immediately they sprang up, because they had no depth of earth. ⁶ When the sun had risen, they were scorched. Because they had no root, they withered away. ⁷ Others fell among thorns. The thorns grew up and choked them. ⁸ Others fell on good soil and yielded fruit: some one hundred times as much, some sixty, and some thirty. ⁹ He who has ears to hear, let him hear." ¹⁸ "Hear, then, the parable of the farmer. ¹⁹ When anyone hears the word of the Kingdom and doesn't understand it, the evil one comes and snatches away that which has been sown in his heart. This is what was sown by the roadside. ²⁰ What was sown on the rocky places, this is he who hears the word and immediately with joy receives it; ²¹ yet he has no root in himself, but endures for a while. When oppression or persecution arises because of the word, immediately he stumbles. ²² What was sown among the thorns, this is he who hears the word, but the cares of this age and the deceitfulness of riches choke the word, and he becomes unfruitful. ²³ What was sown on the good ground, this is he who hears the word and understands it, who most certainly bears fruit and produces, some one hundred times as much, some sixty, and some thirty."

What insight does God give us about applying our hearts to understand what He is saying in Scripture?

What distractions are noted in this text that might tempt someone to not apply their heart to spiritual understanding?

Take a minute and ask the Lord how He wants you to apply this Scripture to your life going forward (and we'll go around the room)?

#8 Proverbs 5:1-10 (WEB)

My son, pay attention to my wisdom. Turn your ear to my understanding, ²that you may maintain discretion, that your lips may preserve knowledge. ³For the lips of an adulteress drip honey. Her mouth is smoother than oil, ⁴but in the end she is as bitter as wormwood, and as sharp as a two-edged sword. ⁵Her feet go down to death. Her steps lead straight to Sheol. ⁶She gives no thought to the way of life. Her ways are crooked, and she doesn't know it. ⁷Now therefore, my sons, listen to me. Don't depart from the words of my mouth. ⁸Remove your way far from her. Don't come near the door of her house, ⁹lest you give your honor to others, and your years to the cruel one; ¹⁰lest strangers feast on your wealth, and your labors enrich another man's house.

What insight does God give us about applying our hearts to understand what He is saying in Scripture?

What distractions are noted in this text that might tempt someone to not apply their heart to spiritual understanding?

Take a minute and ask the Lord how He wants you to apply this Scripture to your life going forward (and we'll go around the room)?

#9 Proverbs 16:16-25 (WEB)

How much better it is to get wisdom than gold! Yes, to get understanding is to be chosen rather than silver. ¹⁷ The highway of the upright is to depart from evil. He who keeps his way preserves his soul. ¹⁸ Pride goes before destruction, and an arrogant spirit before a fall. ¹⁹ It is better to be of a lowly spirit with the poor, than to divide the plunder with the proud. ²⁰ He who heeds the Word finds prosperity. Whoever trusts in Yahweh is blessed. ²¹ The wise in heart shall be called prudent. Pleasantness of the lips promotes instruction. ²² Understanding is a fountain of life to one who has it, but the punishment of fools is their folly. ²³ The heart of the wise instructs his mouth, and adds learning to his lips. ²⁴ Pleasant words are a honeycomb, sweet to the soul, and health to the bones. ²⁵ There is a way which seems right to a man, but in the end it leads to death.

What insight does God give us about applying our hearts to understand what He is saying in Scripture?

What distractions are noted in this text that might tempt someone to not apply their heart to spiritual understanding?

Take a minute and ask the Lord how He wants you to apply this Scripture to your life going forward (and we'll go around the room)?

#10   Matthew 13:10-17 (NASB1995)

And the disciples came and said to Him, "Why do You speak to them in parables?" [11] Jesus answered them, "To you it has been granted to know the mysteries of the kingdom of heaven, but to them it has not been granted. [12] For whoever has, to him *more* shall be given, and he will have an abundance; but whoever does not have, even what he has shall be taken away from him. [13] Therefore I speak to them in parables; because while seeing they do not see, and while hearing they do not hear, nor do they understand. [14] In their case the prophecy of Isaiah is being fulfilled, which says, 'You will keep on hearing, but will not understand; You will keep on seeing, but will not perceive; [15] For the heart of this people has become dull, with their ears they scarcely hear, and they have closed their eyes, otherwise they would see with their eyes, hear with their ears, and understand with their heart and return, and I would heal them.' [16] But blessed are your eyes, because they see; and your ears, because they hear. [17] For truly I say to you that many prophets and righteous men desired to see what you see, and did not see *it*, and to hear what you hear, and did not hear *it*.

What insight does God give us about applying our hearts to understand what He is saying in Scripture?

What distractions are noted in this text that might tempt someone to not apply their heart to spiritual understanding?

Take a minute and ask the Lord how He wants you to apply this Scripture to your life going forward (and we'll go around the room)?

#11 Proverbs 8:1-21 (WEB)

Does not wisdom cry out, and understanding lift up her voice? ²She takes her stand on the top of the high hill, beside the way, where the paths meet. ³She cries out by the gates, at the entry of the city, at the entrance of the doors: ⁴"To you, O men, I call, and my voice *is* to the sons of men. ⁵O you simple ones, understand prudence, and you fools, be of an understanding heart. ⁶Listen, for I will speak of excellent things, and from the opening of my lips *will come* right things; ⁷For my mouth will speak truth; wickedness *is* an abomination to my lips. ⁸All the words of my mouth *are* with righteousness; nothing crooked or perverse *is* in them. ⁹They *are* all plain to him who understands, and right to those who find knowledge. ¹⁰Receive my instruction, and not silver, and knowledge rather than choice gold; ¹¹For wisdom *is* better than rubies, and all the things one may desire cannot be compared with her. ¹²"I, wisdom, dwell with prudence, and find out knowledge *and* discretion. ¹³The fear of the Lord *is* to hate evil; pride and arrogance and the evil way and the perverse mouth I hate. ¹⁴Counsel *is* mine, and sound wisdom; I *am* understanding, I have strength. ¹⁵By me kings reign, and rulers decree justice. ¹⁶By me princes rule, and nobles, all the judges of the earth. ¹⁷I love those who love me, and those who seek me diligently will find me. ¹⁸Riches and honor *are* with me, enduring riches and righteousness. ¹⁹My fruit *is* better than gold, yes, than fine gold, and my revenue than choice silver. ²⁰I traverse the way of righteousness, in the midst of the paths of justice, ²¹That I may cause those who love me to inherit wealth, that I may fill their treasuries.

What insight does God give us about applying our hearts to understand what He is saying in Scripture?

What distractions are noted in this text that might tempt someone to not apply their heart to spiritual understanding?

Take a minute and ask the Lord how He wants you to apply this Scripture to your life going forward (and we'll go around the room)?

#12   Proverbs 9 (WEB)

Wisdom has built her house. She has carved out her seven pillars. ²She has prepared her meat. She has mixed her wine. She has also set her table. ³She has sent out her maidens. She cries from the highest places of the city: ⁴"Whoever is simple, let him turn in here!" As for him who is void of understanding, she says to him, ⁵"Come, eat some of my bread, drink some of the wine which I have mixed! ⁶Leave your simple ways, and live. Walk in the way of understanding." ⁷One who corrects a mocker invites insult. One who reproves a wicked man invites abuse. ⁸Don't reprove a scoffer, lest he hate you. Reprove a wise person, and he will love you. ⁹Instruct a wise person, and he will be still wiser. Teach a righteous person, and he will increase in learning. ¹⁰The fear of Yahweh is the beginning of wisdom. The knowledge of the Holy One is understanding. ¹¹For by me your days will be multiplied. The years of your life will be increased. ¹²If you are wise, you are wise for yourself. If you mock, you alone will bear it. ¹³The foolish woman is loud, undisciplined, and knows nothing. ¹⁴She sits at the door of her house, on a seat in the high places of the city, ¹⁵to call to those who pass by, who go straight on their ways, ¹⁶"Whoever is simple, let him turn in here." as for him who is void of understanding, she says to him, ¹⁷"Stolen water is sweet. Food eaten in secret is pleasant." ¹⁸But he doesn't know that the departed spirits are there, that her guests are in the depths of Sheol.

What insight does God give us about applying our hearts to understand what He is saying in Scripture?

What distractions are noted in this text that might tempt someone to not apply their heart to spiritual understanding?

Take a minute and ask the Lord how He wants you to apply this Scripture to your life going forward (and we'll go around the room)?

#13   Proverbs 10:15-23 (NASB1995)

The rich man's wealth is his fortress,
The ruin of the poor is their poverty.
[16] The wages of the righteous is life,
The income of the wicked, punishment.
[17] He is *on* the path of life who heeds instruction,
But he who ignores reproof goes astray.
[18] He who conceals hatred *has* lying lips,
And he who spreads slander is a fool.
[19] When there are many words, transgression is unavoidable,
But he who restrains his lips is wise.
[20] The tongue of the righteous is *as* choice silver,
The heart of the wicked is *worth* little.
[21] The lips of the righteous feed many,
But fools die for lack of understanding.
[22] It is the blessing of the Lord that makes rich,
And He adds no sorrow to it.
[23] Doing wickedness is like sport to a fool,
And *so is* wisdom to a man of understanding.

What insight does God give us about applying our hearts to understand what He is saying in Scripture?

What distractions are noted in this text that might tempt someone to not apply their heart to spiritual understanding?

Take a minute and ask the Lord how He wants you to apply this Scripture to your life going forward (and we'll go around the room)?

#14   Proverbs 14:26-35 (NASB1995)

In the fear of the Lord there is strong confidence,
And his children will have refuge.
27 The fear of the Lord is a fountain of life,
That one may avoid the snares of death.
28 In a multitude of people is a king's glory,
But in the dearth of people is a prince's ruin.
29 He who is slow to anger has great understanding,
But he who is quick-tempered exalts folly.
30 A tranquil heart is life to the body,
But passion is rottenness to the bones.
31 He who oppresses the poor taunts his Maker,
But he who is gracious to the needy honors Him.
32 The wicked is thrust down by his wrongdoing,
But the righteous has a refuge when he dies.
33 Wisdom rests in the heart of one who has understanding,
But in the hearts of fools it is made known.
34 Righteousness exalts a nation,
But sin is a disgrace to *any* people.
35 The king's favor is toward a servant who acts wisely,
But his anger is toward him who acts shamefully.

What insight does God give us about applying our hearts to understand what He is saying in Scripture?

What distractions are noted in this text that might tempt someone to not apply their heart to spiritual understanding?

Take a minute and ask the Lord how He wants you to apply this Scripture to your life going forward (and we'll go around the room)?

#15   Proverbs 17:16-28 (WEB)

Why is there money in the hand of a fool to buy wisdom, since he has no understanding? ¹⁷ A friend loves at all times; and a brother is born for adversity. ¹⁸ A man void of understanding strikes hands, and becomes collateral in the presence of his neighbor. ¹⁹ He who loves disobedience loves strife. One who builds a high gate seeks destruction. ²⁰ One who has a perverse heart doesn't find prosperity, and one who has a deceitful tongue falls into trouble. ²¹ He who becomes the father of a fool grieves. The father of a fool has no joy. ²² A cheerful heart makes good medicine, but a crushed spirit dries up the bones. ²³ A wicked man receives a bribe in secret, to pervert the ways of justice. ²⁴ Wisdom is before the face of one who has understanding, but the eyes of a fool wander to the ends of the earth. ²⁵ A foolish son brings grief to his father, and bitterness to her who bore him. ²⁶ Also to punish the righteous is not good, nor to flog officials for their integrity. ²⁷ He who spares his words has knowledge. He who is even tempered is a man of understanding. ²⁸ Even a fool, when he keeps silent, is counted wise. When he shuts his lips, he is thought to be discerning.

What insight does God give us about applying our hearts to understand what He is saying in Scripture?

What distractions are noted in this text that might tempt someone to not apply their heart to spiritual understanding?

Take a minute and ask the Lord how He wants you to apply this Scripture to your life going forward (and we'll go around the room)?

#16 Proverbs 15:11-22 ^(WEB)

Sheol and Abaddon are before Yahweh— how much more then the hearts of the children of men! ¹² A scoffer doesn't love to be reproved; he will not go to the wise. ¹³ A glad heart makes a cheerful face, but an aching heart breaks the spirit. ¹⁴ The heart of one who has understanding seeks knowledge, but the mouths of fools feed on folly. ¹⁵ All the days of the afflicted are wretched, but one who has a cheerful heart enjoys a continual feast. ¹⁶ Better is little, with the fear of Yahweh, than great treasure with trouble. ¹⁷ Better is a dinner of herbs, where love is, than a fattened calf with hatred. ¹⁸ A wrathful man stirs up contention, but one who is slow to anger appeases strife. ¹⁹ The way of the sluggard is like a thorn patch, but the path of the upright is a highway. ²⁰ A wise son makes a father glad, but a foolish man despises his mother. ²¹ Folly is joy to one who is void of wisdom, but a man of understanding keeps his way straight. ²² Where there is no counsel, plans fail; but in a multitude of counselors they are established.

What insight does God give us about applying our hearts to understand what He is saying in Scripture?

What distractions are noted in this text that might tempt someone to not apply their heart to spiritual understanding?

Take a minute and ask the Lord how He wants you to apply this Scripture to your life going forward (and we'll go around the room)?

#17   Proverbs 18:10-15 {ESV}

The name of the Lord is a strong tower; the righteous man runs into it and is safe. ¹¹A rich man's wealth is his strong city, and like a high wall in his imagination. ¹²Before destruction a man's heart is haughty, but humility comes before honor. ¹³If one gives an answer before he hears, it is his folly and shame. ¹⁴A man's spirit will endure sickness, but a crushed spirit who can bear? ¹⁵An intelligent heart acquires knowledge, and the ear of the wise seeks knowledge.

What insight does God give us about applying our hearts to understand what He is saying in Scripture?

What distractions are noted in this text that might tempt someone to not apply their heart to spiritual understanding?

Take a minute and ask the Lord how He wants you to apply this Scripture to your life going forward (and we'll go around the room)?

#18 Proverbs 19:1-8 (NKJV)

Better *is* the poor who walks in his integrity than *one who is* perverse in his lips, and is a fool. ²Also it is not good *for* a soul *to be* without knowledge, and he sins who hastens with *his* feet. ³The foolishness of a man twists his way, and his heart frets against the Lord. ⁴Wealth makes many friends, but the poor is separated from his friend. ⁵A false witness will not go unpunished, and *he who* speaks lies will not escape. ⁶Many entreat the favor of the nobility, and every man *is* a friend to one who gives gifts. ⁷All the brothers of the poor hate him; how much more do his friends go far from him! He may pursue *them with* words, *yet* they abandon *him*. ⁸He who gets wisdom loves his own soul; He who keeps understanding will find good.

What insight does God give us about applying our hearts to understand what He is saying in Scripture?

What distractions are noted in this text that might tempt someone to not apply their heart to spiritual understanding?

Take a minute and ask the Lord how He wants you to apply this Scripture to your life going forward (and we'll go around the room)?

#19   Proverbs 22:17-29 (NASB1995)

Incline your ear and hear the words of the wise, and apply your mind to my knowledge; ¹⁸ For it will be pleasant if you keep them within you, that they may be ready on your lips. ¹⁹ So that your trust may be in the Lord, I have taught you today, even you. ²⁰ Have I not written to you excellent things of counsels and knowledge, ²¹ To make you know the certainty of the words of truth that you may correctly answer him who sent you? ²² Do not rob the poor because he is poor, or crush the afflicted at the gate; ²³ For the Lord will plead their case and take the life of those who rob them. ²⁴ Do not associate with a man *given* to anger; or go with a hot-tempered man, ²⁵ Or you will learn his ways and find a snare for yourself. ²⁶ Do not be among those who give pledges, among those who become guarantors for debts. ²⁷ If you have nothing with which to pay, why should he take your bed from under you? ²⁸ Do not move the ancient boundary which your fathers have set. ²⁹ Do you see a man skilled in his work? He will stand before kings; he will not stand before obscure men.

What insight does God give us about applying our hearts to understand what He is saying in Scripture?

What distractions are noted in this text that might tempt someone to not apply their heart to spiritual understanding?

Take a minute and ask the Lord how He wants you to apply this Scripture to your life going forward (and we'll go around the room)?

#20   Proverbs 23:12-23 (NKJV)

Apply your heart to instruction, And your ears to words of knowledge. [13] Do not withhold correction from a child, For *if* you beat him with a rod, he will not die. [14] You shall beat him with a rod, And deliver his soul from hell. [15] My son, if your heart is wise, My heart will rejoice— indeed, I myself; [16] Yes, my inmost being will rejoice When your lips speak right things. [17] Do not let your heart envy sinners, But *be zealous* for the fear of the Lord all the day; [18] For surely there is a hereafter, And your hope will not be cut off. [19] Hear, my son, and be wise; And guide your heart in the way. [20] Do not mix with winebibbers, *Or* with gluttonous eaters of meat; [21] For the drunkard and the glutton will come to poverty, And drowsiness will clothe *a man* with rags. [22] Listen to your father who begot you, And do not despise your mother when she is old. [23] Buy the truth, and do not sell *it, Also* wisdom and instruction and understanding.

What insight does God give us about applying our hearts to understand what He is saying in Scripture?

What distractions are noted in this text that might tempt someone to not apply their heart to spiritual understanding?

Take a minute and ask the Lord how He wants you to apply this Scripture to your life going forward (and we'll go around the room)?

#21   Proverbs 24:1-11 (NKJV)

Don't be envious of evil men, neither desire to be with them; ²for their hearts plot violence and their lips talk about mischief. ³Through wisdom a house is built; by understanding it is established; ⁴by knowledge the rooms are filled with all rare and beautiful treasure. ⁵A wise man has great power; and a knowledgeable man increases strength; ⁶for by wise guidance you wage your war; and victory is in many advisors. ⁷Wisdom is too high for a fool. He doesn't open his mouth in the gate. ⁸One who plots to do evil will be called a schemer. ⁹The schemes of folly are sin. The mocker is detested by men. ¹⁰If you falter in the time of trouble, your strength is small. ¹¹Rescue those who are being led away to death! Indeed, hold back those who are staggering to the slaughter!

What insight does God give us about applying our hearts to understand what He is saying in Scripture?

What distractions are noted in this text that might tempt someone to not apply their heart to spiritual understanding?

Take a minute and ask the Lord how He wants you to apply this Scripture to your life going forward (and we'll go around the room)?

#22 Proverbs 28:1-15 (WEB)

The wicked flee when no one pursues; but the righteous are as bold as a lion. ²In rebellion, a land has many rulers, but order is maintained by a man of understanding and knowledge. ³A needy man who oppresses the poor is like a driving rain which leaves no crops. ⁴Those who forsake the law praise the wicked; but those who keep the law contend with them. ⁵Evil men don't understand justice; but those who seek Yahweh understand it fully. ⁶Better is the poor who walks in his integrity, than he who is perverse in his ways, and he is rich. ⁷Whoever keeps the law is a wise son; but he who is a companion of gluttons shames his father. ⁸He who increases his wealth by excessive interest gathers it for one who has pity on the poor. ⁹He who turns away his ear from hearing the law, even his prayer is an abomination. ¹⁰Whoever causes the upright to go astray in an evil way, he will fall into his own trap; but the blameless will inherit good. ¹¹The rich man is wise in his own eyes; but the poor who has understanding sees through him. ¹²When the righteous triumph, there is great glory; but when the wicked rise, men hide themselves. ¹³He who conceals his sins doesn't prosper, but whoever confesses and renounces them finds mercy. ¹⁴Blessed is the man who always fears; but one who hardens his heart falls into trouble. ¹⁵As a roaring lion or a charging bear, so is a wicked ruler over helpless people.

What insight does God give us about applying our hearts to understand what He is saying in Scripture?

What distractions are noted in this text that might tempt someone to not apply their heart to spiritual understanding?

Take a minute and ask the Lord how He wants you to apply this Scripture to your life going forward (and we'll go around the room)?

For further learning

#23   Proverbs 24:12-22 (WEB)

If you say, "Behold, we didn't know this," doesn't he who weighs the hearts consider it? He who keeps your soul, doesn't he know it? Shall he not render to every man according to his work? [13] My son, eat honey, for it is good, the droppings of the honeycomb, which are sweet to your taste; [14] so you shall know wisdom to be to your soul. If you have found it, then there will be a reward: Your hope will not be cut off. [15] Do not lie in wait, O wicked *man,* against the dwelling of the righteous; do not plunder his resting place; [16] for a righteous *man* may fall seven times and rise again, but the wicked shall fall by calamity. [17] Do not rejoice when your enemy falls, and do not let your heart be glad when he stumbles; [18] lest the Lord see *it,* and it displease Him, and He turn away His wrath from him. [19] Do not fret because of evildoers, nor be envious of the wicked; [20] for there will be no prospect for the evil *man;* the lamp of the wicked will be put out. [21] My son, fear the Lord and the king; do not associate with those given to change; [22] for their calamity will rise suddenly, and who knows the ruin those two can bring?

What insight does God give us about applying our hearts to understand what He is saying in Scripture?

Take a minute and ask the Lord how He wants you to apply this Scripture to your life going forward (and we'll go around the room)?

#24   Proverbs 28:16-28 (WEB)

A tyrannical ruler lacks judgment. One who hates ill-gotten gain will have long days. ¹⁷ A man who is tormented by life blood will be a fugitive until death; no one will support him. ¹⁸ Whoever walks blamelessly is kept safe; but one with perverse ways will fall suddenly. ¹⁹ One who works his land will have an abundance of food; but one who chases fantasies will have his fill of poverty. ²⁰ A faithful man is rich with blessings; but one who is eager to be rich will not go unpunished. ²¹ To show partiality is not good; yet a man will do wrong for a piece of bread. ²² A stingy man hurries after riches, and doesn't know that poverty waits for him. ²³ One who rebukes a man will afterward find more favor than one who flatters with the tongue. ²⁴ Whoever robs his father or his mother and says, "It's not wrong," is a partner with a destroyer. ²⁵ One who is greedy stirs up strife; but one who trusts in Yahweh will prosper. ²⁶ One who trusts in himself is a fool; but one who walks in wisdom is kept safe. ²⁷ One who gives to the poor has no lack; but one who closes his eyes will have many curses. ²⁸ When the wicked rise, men hide themselves; but when they perish, the righteous thrive.

What insight does God give us about applying our hearts to understand what He is saying in Scripture?

Take a minute and ask the Lord how He wants you to apply this Scripture to your life going forward (and we'll go around the room)?

#25   Ecclesiastes 7:8-14 (NASB1995)

The end of a matter is better than its beginning; patience of spirit is better than haughtiness of spirit. ⁹ Do not be eager in your heart to be angry, for anger resides in the bosom of fools. ¹⁰ Do not say, "Why is it that the former days were better than these?" For it is not from wisdom that you ask about this. ¹¹ Wisdom along with an inheritance is good and an advantage to those who see the sun. ¹² For wisdom is protection *just as* money is protection, but the advantage of knowledge is that wisdom preserves the lives of its possessors. ¹³ Consider the work of God, for who is able to straighten what He has bent? ¹⁴ In the day of prosperity be happy, but in the day of adversity consider—God has made the one as well as the other so that man will not discover anything *that will be* after him.

What insight does God give us about applying our hearts to understand what He is saying in Scripture?

Take a minute and ask the Lord how He wants you to apply this Scripture to your life going forward (and we'll go around the room)?

#26   Ecclesiastes 7:15-29 (AMPC)

I have seen everything in the days of my vanity (my emptiness, falsity, vainglory, and futility): there is a righteous man who perishes in his righteousness, and there is a wicked man who prolongs his life in [spite of] his evildoing. 16 Be not [morbidly exacting and externally] righteous overmuch, neither strive to make yourself [pretentiously appear] overwise—why should you [get puffed up and] destroy yourself [with presumptuous self-sufficiency]? 17 [Although all have sinned] be not wicked overmuch *or* willfully, neither be foolish—why should you die before your time? 18 It is good that you should take hold of this and from that withdraw not your hand; for he who [reverently] fears *and* worships God will come forth from them all. 19 [True] wisdom is a strength to the wise man more than ten rulers *or* valiant generals who are in the city. 20 Surely there is not a righteous man upon earth who does good and never sins. 21 Do not give heed to everything that is said, lest you hear your servant cursing you— 22 For often your own heart knows that you have likewise cursed others. 23 All this have I tried *and* proved by wisdom. I said, I will be wise [independently of God]—but it was far from me. 24 That which is is far off, and that which is deep is very deep—who can find it out [true wisdom independent of the fear of God]? 25 I turned about [penitent] and my heart was set to know and to search out and to seek [true] wisdom and the reason of things, and to know that wickedness is folly and that foolishness is madness [and what had led me into such wickedness and madness]. 26 And I found that [of all sinful follies none has been so ruinous in seducing one away from God as idolatrous women] more bitter than death is the woman whose heart is snares and nets and whose hands are bands. Whoever pleases God shall escape from her, but the sinner shall be taken by her. 27 Behold, this I have found, says the Preacher, while weighing one thing after another to find out the right estimate [and the reason]— 28 Which I am still seeking but have not found—one upright man among a thousand have I found, but an upright woman among all those [one thousand in my harem] have I not found. ²⁹ Behold, this is the only [reason for it that] I have found: God made man upright, but they [men and women] have sought out many devices [for evil].

What insight does God give us about applying our hearts to understand what He is saying in Scripture?

Take a minute and ask the Lord how He wants you to apply this Scripture to your life going forward (and we'll go around the room)?

#27   Mark 12:28-40 (WEB)

One of the scribes came, and heard them questioning together, and knowing that he had answered them well, asked him, "Which commandment is the greatest of all?" ²⁹ Jesus answered, "The greatest is, 'Hear, Israel, the Lord our God, the Lord is one: ³⁰ you shall love the Lord your God with all your heart, and with all your soul, and with all your mind, and with all your strength.' Deuteronomy 6:4-5 This is the first commandment. ³¹ The second is like this, 'You shall love your neighbor as yourself.' Leviticus 19:18 There is no other commandment greater than these." ³² The scribe said to him, "Truly, teacher, you have said well that he is one, and there is none other but he, ³³ and to love him with all the heart, and with all the understanding, with all the soul, and with all the strength, and to love his neighbor as himself, is more important than all whole burnt offerings and sacrifices." ³⁴ When Jesus saw that he answered wisely, he said to him, "You are not far from God's Kingdom." No one dared ask him any question after that. ³⁵ Jesus responded, as he taught in the temple, "How is it that the scribes say that the Christ is the son of David? ³⁶ For David himself said in the Holy Spirit, 'The Lord said to my Lord, "Sit at my right hand, until I make your enemies the footstool of your feet."' Psalm 110:1 ³⁷ Therefore David himself calls him Lord, so how can he be his son?" The common people heard him gladly. ³⁸ In his teaching he said to them, "Beware of the scribes, who like to walk in long robes, and to get greetings in the marketplaces, ³⁹ and the best seats in the synagogues, and the best places at feasts: ⁴⁰ those who devour widows' houses, and for a pretense make long prayers. These will receive greater condemnation."

What insight does God give us about applying our hearts to understand what He is saying in Scripture?

Take a minute and ask the Lord how He wants you to apply this Scripture to your life going forward (and we'll go around the room)?

#28 Romans 12:1-9 (AMPC)

I appeal to you therefore, brethren, *and* beg of you in view of [all] the mercies of God, to make a decisive dedication of your bodies [presenting all your members and faculties] as a living sacrifice, holy (devoted, consecrated) and well pleasing to God, which is your reasonable (rational, intelligent) service *and* spiritual worship. ²Do not be conformed to this world (this age), [fashioned after and adapted to its external, superficial customs], but be transformed (changed) by the [entire] renewal of your mind [by its new ideals and its new attitude], so that you may prove [for yourselves] what is the good and acceptable and perfect will of God, *even* the thing which is good and acceptable and perfect [in His sight for you]. ³For by the grace (unmerited favor of God) given to me I warn everyone among you not to estimate *and* think of himself more highly than he ought [not to have an exaggerated opinion of his own importance], but to rate his ability with sober judgment, each according to the degree of faith apportioned by God to him. ⁴For as in one physical body we have many parts (organs, members) and all of these parts do not have the same function *or* use, ⁵So we, numerous as we are, are one body in Christ (the Messiah) and individually we are parts one of another [mutually dependent on one another]. ⁶Having gifts (faculties, talents, qualities) that differ according to the grace given us, let us use them: [He whose gift is] prophecy, [let him prophesy] according to the proportion of his faith; ⁷[He whose gift is] practical service, let him give himself to serving; he who teaches, to his teaching; ⁸He who exhorts (encourages), to his exhortation; he who contributes, let him do it in simplicity *and* liberality; he who gives aid *and* superintends, with zeal *and* singleness of mind; he who does acts of mercy, with genuine cheerfulness *and* joyful eagerness. ⁹[Let your] love be sincere (a real thing); hate what is evil [loathe all ungodliness, turn in horror from wickedness], but hold fast to that which is good.

What insight does God give us about applying our hearts to understand what He is saying in Scripture?

Take a minute and ask the Lord how He wants you to apply this Scripture to your life going forward (and we'll go around the room)?

#29 Philippians 4:1-13 (WEB)

Therefore, my brothers, beloved and longed for, my joy and crown, stand firm in the Lord in this way, my beloved. ² I exhort Euodia, and I exhort Syntyche, to think the same way in the Lord. ³ Yes, I beg you also, true partner, help these women, for they labored with me in the Good News with Clement also, and the rest of my fellow workers, whose names are in the book of life. ⁴ Rejoice in the Lord always! Again I will say, "Rejoice!" ⁵ Let your gentleness be known to all men. The Lord is at hand. ⁶ In nothing be anxious, but in everything, by prayer and petition with thanksgiving, let your requests be made known to God. ⁷ And the peace of God, which surpasses all understanding, will guard your hearts and your thoughts in Christ Jesus. ⁸ Finally, brothers, whatever things are true, whatever things are honorable, whatever things are just, whatever things are pure, whatever things are lovely, whatever things are of good report: if there is any virtue and if there is any praise, think about these things. ⁹ The things which you learned, received, heard, and saw in me: do these things, and the God of peace will be with you. ¹⁰ But I rejoice in the Lord greatly, that now at length you have revived your thought for me; in which you did indeed take thought, but you lacked opportunity. ¹¹ Not that I speak because of lack, for I have learned in whatever state I am, to be content in it. ¹² I know how to be humbled, and I also know how to abound. In everything and in all things I have learned the secret both to be filled and to be hungry, both to abound and to be in need. ¹³ I can do all things through Christ, who strengthens me.

What insight does God give us about applying our hearts to understand what He is saying in Scripture?

Take a minute and ask the Lord how He wants you to apply this Scripture to your life going forward (and we'll go around the room)?

#30 John 7:14-24 (WEB)

But when it was now the middle of the feast, Jesus went up into the temple and taught. ¹⁵ The Jews therefore marveled, saying, "How does this man know letters, having never been educated?" ¹⁶ Jesus therefore answered them, "My teaching is not mine, but his who sent me. ¹⁷ If anyone desires to do his will, he will know about the teaching, whether it is from God, or if I am speaking from myself. ¹⁸ He who speaks from himself seeks his own glory, but he who seeks the glory of him who sent him is true, and no unrighteousness is in him. ¹⁹ Didn't Moses give you the law, and yet none of you keeps the law? Why do you seek to kill me?" ²⁰ The multitude answered, "You have a demon! Who seeks to kill you?" ²¹ Jesus answered them, "I did one work and you all marvel because of it. ²² Moses has given you circumcision (not that it is of Moses, but of the Fathers), and on the Sabbath you circumcise a boy. ²³ If a boy receives circumcision on the Sabbath, that the law of Moses may not be broken, are you angry with me, because I made a man completely healthy on the Sabbath? ²⁴ Don't judge according to appearance, but judge righteous judgment."

What insight does God give us about applying our hearts to understand what He is saying in Scripture?

Take a minute and ask the Lord how He wants you to apply this Scripture to your life going forward (and we'll go around the room)?

#31 Ephesians 5:15-24 (WEB)

Therefore watch carefully how you walk, not as unwise, but as wise, [16] redeeming the time, because the days are evil. [17] Therefore don't be foolish, but understand what the will of the Lord is. [18] Don't be drunken with wine, in which is dissipation, but be filled with the Spirit, [19] speaking to one another in psalms, hymns, and spiritual songs; singing and making melody in your heart to the Lord; [20] giving thanks always concerning all things in the name of our Lord Jesus Christ, to God, even the Father; [21] subjecting yourselves to one another in the fear of Christ. Wives, be subject to your own husbands, as to the Lord. [23] For the husband is the head of the wife, as Christ also is the head of the assembly, being himself the Savior of the body. [24] But as the assembly is subject to Christ, so let the wives also be to their own husbands in everything.

What insight does God give us about applying our hearts to understand what He is saying in Scripture?

Take a minute and ask the Lord how He wants you to apply this Scripture to your life going forward (and we'll go around the room)?

#32 Proverbs 29:1-15 (WEB)

He who is often rebuked and stiffens his neck will be destroyed suddenly, with no remedy. ²When the righteous thrive, the people rejoice; but when the wicked rule, the people groan. ³Whoever loves wisdom brings joy to his father; but a companion of prostitutes squanders his wealth. ⁴The king by justice makes the land stable, but he who takes bribes tears it down. ⁵A man who flatters his neighbor spreads a net for his feet. ⁶An evil man is snared by his sin, but the righteous can sing and be glad. ⁷The righteous care about justice for the poor. The wicked aren't concerned about knowledge. ⁸Mockers stir up a city, but wise men turn away anger. ⁹If a wise man goes to court with a foolish man, the fool rages or scoffs, and there is no peace. ¹⁰The bloodthirsty hate a man of integrity; and they seek the life of the upright. ¹¹A fool vents all of his anger, but a wise man brings himself under control. ¹²If a ruler listens to lies, all of his officials are wicked. ¹³The poor man and the oppressor have this in common: Yahweh gives sight to the eyes of both. ¹⁴The king who fairly judges the poor, his throne shall be established forever. ¹⁵The rod of correction gives wisdom, but a child left to himself causes shame to his mother.

What insight does God give us about applying our hearts to understand what He is saying in Scripture?

Take a minute and ask the Lord how He wants you to apply this Scripture to your life going forward (and we'll go around the room)?

#33 Colossians 3:12-17 (NKJV)

Therefore, as *the* elect of God, holy and beloved, put on tender mercies, kindness, humility, meekness, longsuffering; ¹³ bearing with one another, and forgiving one another, if anyone has a complaint against another; even as Christ forgave you, so you also *must do.* ¹⁴ But above all these things put on love, which is the bond of perfection. ¹⁵ And let the peace of God rule in your hearts, to which also you were called in one body; and be thankful. ¹⁶ Let the word of Christ dwell in you richly in all wisdom, teaching and admonishing one another in psalms and hymns and spiritual songs, singing with grace in your hearts to the Lord. ¹⁷ And whatever you do in word or deed, *do* all in the name of the Lord Jesus, giving thanks to God the Father through Him.

What insight does God give us about applying our hearts to understand what He is saying in Scripture?

Take a minute and ask the Lord how He wants you to apply this Scripture to your life going forward (and we'll go around the room)?

#34 Daniel 1:15-21 (WEB)

At the end of ten days, their faces appeared fairer, and they were fatter in flesh, than all the youths who ate of the king's dainties. [16] So the steward took away their dainties, and the wine that they were given to drink, and gave them vegetables. [17] Now as for these four youths, God gave them knowledge and skill in all learning and wisdom; and Daniel had understanding in all visions and dreams. [18] At the end of the days which the king had appointed for bringing them in, the prince of the eunuchs brought them in before Nebuchadnezzar. [19] The king talked with them; and among them all was found no one like Daniel, Hananiah, Mishael, and Azariah. Therefore stood they before the king. [20] In every matter of wisdom and understanding, concerning which the king inquired of them, he found them ten times better than all the magicians and enchanters who were in all his realm. [21] Daniel continued even to the first year of king Cyrus.

What insight does God give us about applying our hearts to understand what He is saying in Scripture?

Take a minute and ask the Lord how He wants you to apply this Scripture to your life going forward (and we'll go around the room)?

#35   Matthew 11:25-30 ^(NASB1995)

At that time Jesus said, "I praise You, Father, Lord of heaven and earth, that You have hidden these things from *the* wise and intelligent and have revealed them to infants. ²⁶ Yes, Father, for this way was well-pleasing in Your sight. ²⁷ All things have been handed over to Me by My Father; and no one knows the Son except the Father; nor does anyone know the Father except the Son, and anyone to whom the Son wills to reveal *Him*. ²⁸ "Come to Me, all who are weary and heavy-laden, and I will give you rest. ²⁹ Take My yoke upon you and learn from Me, for I am gentle and humble in heart, and you will find rest for your souls. ³⁰ For My yoke is easy and My burden is light."

What insight does God give us about applying our hearts to understand what He is saying in Scripture?

Take a minute and ask the Lord how He wants you to apply this Scripture to your life going forward (and we'll go around the room)?

#36 1 Corinthians 1:18-31 (WEB)

For the word of the cross is foolishness to those who are dying, but to us who are being saved it is the power of God. [19] For it is written, "I will destroy the wisdom of the wise. I will bring the discernment of the discerning to nothing." Isaiah 29:14 [20] Where is the wise? Where is the scribe? Where is the lawyer of this world? Hasn't God made foolish the wisdom of this world? [21] For seeing that in the wisdom of God, the world through its wisdom didn't know God, it was God's good pleasure through the foolishness of the preaching to save those who believe. [22] For Jews ask for signs, Greeks seek after wisdom, [23] but we preach Christ crucified: a stumbling block to Jews, and foolishness to Greeks, [24] but to those who are called, both Jews and Greeks, Christ is the power of God and the wisdom of God; [25] because the foolishness of God is wiser than men, and the weakness of God is stronger than men. [26] For you see your calling, brothers, that not many are wise according to the flesh, not many mighty, and not many noble; [27] but God chose the foolish things of the world that he might put to shame those who are wise. God chose the weak things of the world that he might put to shame the things that are strong. [28] God chose the lowly things of the world, and the things that are despised, and the things that don't exist, that he might bring to nothing the things that exist, [29] that no flesh should boast before God. [30] Because of him, you are in Christ Jesus, who was made to us wisdom from God, and righteousness and sanctification, and redemption: [31] that, as it is written, "He who boasts, let him boast in the Lord." Jeremiah 9:24

What insight does God give us about applying our hearts to understand what He is saying in Scripture?

Take a minute and ask the Lord how He wants you to apply this Scripture to your life going forward (and we'll go around the room)?

#37   Ephesians 1:15-2:3 (NKJV)

Therefore I also, after I heard of your faith in the Lord Jesus and your love for all the saints, [16] do not cease to give thanks for you, making mention of you in my prayers: [17] that the God of our Lord Jesus Christ, the Father of glory, may give to you the spirit of wisdom and revelation in the knowledge of Him, [18] the eyes of your understanding being enlightened; that you may know what is the hope of His calling, what are the riches of the glory of His inheritance in the saints, [19] and what *is* the exceeding greatness of His power toward us who believe, according to the working of His mighty power [20] which He worked in Christ when He raised Him from the dead and seated *Him* at His right hand in the heavenly *places,* [21] far above all principality and power and might and dominion, and every name that is named, not only in this age but also in that which is to come. [22] And He put all *things* under His feet, and gave Him *to be* head over all *things* to the church, [23] which is His body, the fullness of Him who fills all in all. [2:1] And you *He made alive,* who were dead in trespasses and sins, [2] in which you once walked according to the course of this world, according to the prince of the power of the air, the spirit who now works in the sons of disobedience, [3] among whom also we all once conducted ourselves in the lusts of our flesh, fulfilling the desires of the flesh and of the mind, and were by nature children of wrath, just as the others.

What insight does God give us about applying our hearts to understand what He is saying in Scripture?

Take a minute and ask the Lord how He wants you to apply this Scripture to your life going forward (and we'll go around the room)?

#38 2 Timothy 3 (WEB)

But know this: that in the last days, grievous times will come. ²For men will be lovers of self, lovers of money, boastful, arrogant, blasphemers, disobedient to parents, unthankful, unholy, ³without natural affection, unforgiving, slanderers, without self-control, fierce, not lovers of good, ⁴traitors, headstrong, conceited, lovers of pleasure rather than lovers of God, ⁵holding a form of godliness, but having denied its power. Turn away from these, also. ⁶For some of these are people who creep into houses and take captive gullible women loaded down with sins, led away by various lusts, ⁷always learning, and never able to come to the knowledge of the truth. ⁸Even as Jannes and Jambres opposed Moses, so these also oppose the truth, men corrupted in mind, who concerning the faith are rejected. ⁹But they will proceed no further. For their folly will be evident to all men, as theirs also came to be. ¹⁰But you followed my teaching, conduct, purpose, faith, patience, love, steadfastness, ¹¹persecutions, and sufferings: those things that happened to me at Antioch, Iconium, and Lystra. I endured those persecutions. The Lord delivered me out of them all. ¹²Yes, and all who desire to live godly in Christ Jesus will suffer persecution. ¹³But evil men and impostors will grow worse and worse, deceiving and being deceived. ¹⁴But you remain in the things which you have learned and have been assured of, knowing from whom you have learned them. ¹⁵From infancy, you have known the holy Scriptures which are able to make you wise for salvation through faith, which is in Christ Jesus. ¹⁶Every Scripture is God-breathed and profitable for teaching, for reproof, for correction, and for instruction in righteousness, ¹⁷that each person who belongs to God may be complete, thoroughly equipped for every good work.

What insight does God give us about applying our hearts to understand what He is saying in Scripture?

Take a minute and ask the Lord how He wants you to apply this Scripture to your life going forward (and we'll go around the room)?

#39   James 3 (WEB)

Let not many of you be teachers, my brothers, knowing that we will receive heavier judgment. ²For we all stumble in many things. Anyone who doesn't stumble in word is a perfect person, able to bridle the whole body also. ³Indeed, we put bits into the horses' mouths so that they may obey us, and we guide their whole body. ⁴Behold, the ships also, though they are so big and are driven by fierce winds, are yet guided by a very small rudder, wherever the pilot desires. ⁵So the tongue is also a little member, and boasts great things. See how a small fire can spread to a large forest! ⁶And the tongue is a fire. The world of iniquity among our members is the tongue, which defiles the whole body, and sets on fire the course of nature, and is set on fire by Gehenna. ⁷For every kind of animal, bird, creeping thing, and sea creature, is tamed, and has been tamed by mankind; ⁸but nobody can tame the tongue. It is a restless evil, full of deadly poison. ⁹With it we bless our God and Father, and with it we curse men who are made in the image of God. ¹⁰Out of the same mouth comes blessing and cursing. My brothers, these things ought not to be so. ¹¹Does a spring send out from the same opening fresh and bitter water? ¹²Can a fig tree, my brothers, yield olives, or a vine figs? Thus no spring yields both salt water and fresh water. ¹³Who is wise and understanding among you? Let him show by his good conduct that his deeds are done in gentleness of wisdom. ¹⁴But if you have bitter jealousy and selfish ambition in your heart, don't boast and don't lie against the truth. ¹⁵This wisdom is not that which comes down from above, but is earthly, sensual, and demonic. ¹⁶For where jealousy and selfish ambition are, there is confusion and every evil deed. ¹⁷But the wisdom that is from above is first pure, then peaceful, gentle, reasonable, full of mercy and good fruits, without partiality, and without hypocrisy. ¹⁸Now the fruit of righteousness is sown in peace by those who make peace.

What insight does God give us about applying our hearts to understand what He is saying in Scripture?

Take a minute and ask the Lord how He wants you to apply this Scripture to your life going forward (and we'll go around the room)?

#40   Ecclesiastes 10 (AMPC)

Dead flies cause the ointment of the perfumer to putrefy [and] send forth a vile odor; so does a little folly [in him who is valued for wisdom] outweigh wisdom and honor. ²A wise man's heart turns him toward his right hand, but a fool's heart toward his left. ³Even when he who is a fool walks along the road, his heart *and* understanding fail him, and he says of everyone *and* to everyone that he is a fool. ⁴If the temper of the ruler rises up against you, do not leave your place [or show a resisting spirit]; for gentleness *and* calmness prevent *or* put a stop to great offenses. ⁵There is an evil which I have seen under the sun, like an error which proceeds from the ruler: ⁶Folly is set in great dignity *and* in high places, and the rich sit in low places. ⁷I have seen slaves on horses, and princes walking like slaves on the earth. ⁸He who digs a pit [for others] will fall into it, and whoever breaks through a fence *or* a [stone] wall, a serpent will bite him. ⁹Whoever removes [landmark] stones *or* hews out [new ones with similar intent] will be hurt with them, *and* he who fells trees will be endangered by them. ¹⁰If the ax is dull and the man does not whet the edge, he must put forth more strength; but wisdom helps him to succeed. ¹¹If the serpent bites before it is charmed, then it is no use to call a charmer [and the slanderer is no better than the uncharmed snake]. ¹²The words of a wise man's mouth are gracious *and* win him favor, but the lips of a fool consume him. ¹³The beginning of the words of his mouth is foolishness, and the end of his talk is wicked madness. ¹⁴A fool also multiplies words, though no man can tell what will be—and what will happen after he is gone, who can tell him? ¹⁵The labor of fools wearies every one of them, because [he is so ignorant of the ordinary matters that] he does not even know how to get to town. ¹⁶Woe to you, O land, when your king is a child *or* a servant and when your officials feast in the morning! ¹⁷Happy (fortunate and to be envied) are you, O land, when your king is a free man *and* of noble birth *and* character and when your officials feast at the proper time—for strength and not for drunkenness! [18] Through indolence the rafters [of state affairs] decay *and* the roof sinks in, and through idleness of the hands the house leaks. [19] [Instead of repairing the breaches, the officials] make a feast for laughter, serve wine to cheer life, and [depend on tax] money to answer for all of it. [20] Curse not the king, no, not even in your thoughts, and curse not the rich in your bedchamber, for a bird of the air will carry the voice, and a winged creature will tell the matter.

What insight does God give us about applying our hearts to understand what He is saying in Scripture?

Take a minute and ask the Lord how He wants you to apply this Scripture to your life going forward (and we'll go around the room)?

#41   Colossians 2:1-10 (ESV)

For I want you to know how great a struggle I have for you and for those at Laodicea and for all who have not seen me face to face, ²that their hearts may be encouraged, being knit together in love, to reach all the riches of full assurance of understanding and the knowledge of God's mystery, which is Christ, ³in whom are hidden all the treasures of wisdom and knowledge. ⁴I say this in order that no one may delude you with plausible arguments. ⁵For though I am absent in body, yet I am with you in spirit, rejoicing to see your good order and the firmness of your faith in Christ. ⁶Therefore, as you received Christ Jesus the Lord, so walk in him, ⁷rooted and built up in him and established in the faith, just as you were taught, abounding in thanksgiving. ⁸See to it that no one takes you captive by philosophy and empty deceit, according to human tradition, according to the elemental spirits of the world, and not according to Christ. ⁹For in him the whole fullness of deity dwells bodily, ¹⁰and you have been filled in him, who is the head of all rule and authority.

What insight does God give us about applying our hearts to understand what He is saying in Scripture?

Take a minute and ask the Lord how He wants you to apply this Scripture to your life going forward (and we'll go around the room)?

#42   Ecclesiastes 1:12-18 (AMPC)

I, the Preacher, have been king over Israel in Jerusalem. ¹³And I applied myself by heart *and* mind to seek and search out by [human] wisdom all human activity under heaven. It is a miserable business which God has given to the sons of man with which to busy themselves. ¹⁴I have seen all the works that are done under the sun, and behold, all is vanity, a striving after the wind *and* a feeding on wind. ¹⁵What is crooked cannot be made straight, and what is defective *and* lacking cannot be counted. ¹⁶I entered into counsel with my own mind, saying, Behold, I have acquired great [human] wisdom, yes, more than all who have been over Jerusalem before me; and my mind has had great experience of [moral] wisdom and [scientific] knowledge. ¹⁷And I gave my mind to know [practical] wisdom and to discern [the character of] madness and folly [in which men seem to find satisfaction]; I perceived that this also is a searching after wind *and* a feeding on it. ¹⁸For in much [human] wisdom is much vexation, and he who increases knowledge increases sorrow.

What insight does God give us about applying our hearts to understand what He is saying in Scripture?

Take a minute and ask the Lord how He wants you to apply this Scripture to your life going forward (and we'll go around the room)?

#43   1 John 5:10-21 (WEB)

He who believes in the Son of God has the testimony in himself. He who doesn't believe God has made him a liar, because he has not believed in the testimony that God has given concerning his Son. [11] The testimony is this, that God gave to us eternal life, and this life is in his Son. [12] He who has the Son has the life. He who doesn't have God's Son doesn't have the life. [13] These things I have written to you who believe in the name of the Son of God, that you may know that you have eternal life, and that you may continue to believe in the name of the Son of God. [14] This is the boldness which we have toward him, that if we ask anything according to his will, he listens to us. [15] And if we know that he listens to us, whatever we ask, we know that we have the petitions which we have asked of him. [16] If anyone sees his brother sinning a sin not leading to death, he shall ask, and God will give him life for those who sin not leading to death. There is a sin leading to death. I don't say that he should make a request concerning this. [17] All unrighteousness is sin, and there is a sin not leading to death. [18] We know that whoever is born of God doesn't sin, but he who was born of God keeps himself, and the evil one doesn't touch him. [19] We know that we are of God, and the whole world lies in the power of the evil one. [20] We know that the Son of God has come, and has given us an understanding, that we know him who is true, and we are in him who is true, in his Son Jesus Christ. This is the true God and eternal life. [21] Little children, keep yourselves from idols.

What insight does God give us about applying our hearts to understand what He is saying in Scripture?

Take a minute and ask the Lord how He wants you to apply this Scripture to your life going forward (and we'll go around the room)?

#44   Daniel 2:16-23 (WEB)

Daniel went in, and desired of the king that he would appoint him a time, and he would show the king the interpretation. ¹⁷ Then Daniel went to his house and made the thing known to Hananiah, Mishael, and Azariah, his companions: ¹⁸ that they would desire mercies of the God of heaven concerning this secret; that Daniel and his companions would not perish with the rest of the wise men of Babylon. ¹⁹ Then the secret was revealed to Daniel in a vision of the night. Then Daniel blessed the God of heaven. ²⁰ Daniel answered, "Blessed be the name of God forever and ever; for wisdom and might are his. ²¹ He changes the times and the seasons. He removes kings and sets up kings. He gives wisdom to the wise, and knowledge to those who have understanding. ²² He reveals the deep and secret things. He knows what is in the darkness, and the light dwells with him. ²³ I thank you and praise you, O God of my fathers, who have given me wisdom and might, and have now made known to me what we desired of you; for you have made known to us the king's matter."

What insight does God give us about applying our hearts to understand what He is saying in Scripture?

Take a minute and ask the Lord how He wants you to apply this Scripture to your life going forward (and we'll go around the room)?

#45   Hosea 14 (WEB)

Israel, return to Yahweh your God; for you have fallen because of your sin. ²Take words with you, and return to Yahweh. Tell him, "Forgive all our sins, and accept that which is good: so we offer our lips like bulls. ³Assyria can't save us. We won't ride on horses; neither will we say any more to the work of our hands, 'Our gods!' for in you the fatherless finds mercy." ⁴"I will heal their waywardness. I will love them freely; for my anger is turned away from him. ⁵I will be like the dew to Israel. He will blossom like the lily, and send down his roots like Lebanon. ⁶His branches will spread, and his beauty will be like the olive tree, and his fragrance like Lebanon. ⁷Men will dwell in his shade. They will revive like the grain, and blossom like the vine. Their fragrance will be like the wine of Lebanon. ⁸Ephraim, what have I to do any more with idols? I answer, and will take care of him. I am like a green cypress tree; from me your fruit is found." ⁹Who is wise, that he may understand these things? Who is prudent, that he may know them? For the ways of Yahweh are right, and the righteous walk in them; but the rebellious stumble in them.

What insight does God give us about applying our hearts to understand what He is saying in Scripture?

Take a minute and ask the Lord how He wants you to apply this Scripture to your life going forward (and we'll go around the room)?

#46 Colossians 1:1-14 (NASB1995)

Paul, an apostle of Christ Jesus by the will of God, and Timothy our brother, ²To the saints and faithful brothers *and sisters* in Christ *who are* at Colossae: Grace to you and peace from God our Father. ³We give thanks to God, the Father of our Lord Jesus Christ, praying always for you, ⁴since we heard of your faith in Christ Jesus and the love which you have for all the saints; ⁵because of the hope laid up for you in heaven, of which you previously heard in the word of truth, the gospel ⁶which has come to you, just as in all the world also it is constantly bearing fruit and increasing, even as *it has been doing* in you also since the day you heard *of it* and understood the grace of God in truth; ⁷just as you learned *it* from Epaphras, our beloved fellow bond-servant, who is a faithful servant of Christ on our behalf, ⁸and he also informed us of your love in the Spirit. ⁹For this reason also, since the day we heard *of it*, we have not ceased to pray for you and to ask that you may be filled with the knowledge of His will in all spiritual wisdom and understanding, ¹⁰so that you will walk in a manner worthy of the Lord, to please *Him* in all respects, bearing fruit in every good work and increasing in the knowledge of God; ¹¹strengthened with all power, according to His glorious might, for the attaining of all steadfastness and patience; joyously ¹²giving thanks to the Father, who has qualified us to share in the inheritance of the saints in Light. ¹³For He rescued us from the domain of darkness, and transferred us to the kingdom of His beloved Son, ¹⁴in whom we have redemption, the forgiveness of sins.

What insight does God give us about applying our hearts to understand what He is saying in Scripture?

Take a minute and ask the Lord how He wants you to apply this Scripture to your life going forward (and we'll go around the room)?

#47   2 Timothy 2:1-14 (WEB)

You therefore, my child, be strengthened in the grace that is in Christ Jesus. ²The things which you have heard from me among many witnesses, commit the same things to faithful men, who will be able to teach others also. ³You therefore must endure hardship as a good soldier of Christ Jesus. ⁴No soldier on duty entangles himself in the affairs of life, that he may please him who enrolled him as a soldier. ⁵Also, if anyone competes in athletics, he isn't crowned unless he has competed by the rules. ⁶The farmer who labors must be the first to get a share of the crops. ⁷Consider what I say, and may the Lord give you understanding in all things. ⁸Remember Jesus Christ, risen from the dead, of the offspring of David, according to my Good News, ⁹in which I suffer hardship to the point of chains as a criminal. But God's word isn't chained. ¹⁰Therefore I endure all things for the chosen ones' sake, that they also may obtain the salvation which is in Christ Jesus with eternal glory. ¹¹This saying is trustworthy: "For if we died with him, we will also live with him. ¹²If we endure, we will also reign with him. If we deny him, he also will deny us. ¹³If we are faithless, he remains faithful; for he can't deny himself." ¹⁴Remind them of these things, charging them in the sight of the Lord, that they don't argue about words, to no profit, to the subverting of those who hear.

What insight does God give us about applying our hearts to understand what He is saying in Scripture?

Take a minute and ask the Lord how He wants you to apply this Scripture to your life going forward (and we'll go around the room)?

#48   Proverbs 18:1-9 (ESV)

Whoever isolates himself seeks his own desire; he breaks out against all sound judgment. ²A fool takes no pleasure in understanding, but only in expressing his opinion. ³When wickedness comes, contempt comes also, and with dishonor comes disgrace. ⁴The words of a man's mouth are deep waters; the fountain of wisdom is a bubbling brook. ⁵It is not good to be partial to the wicked or to deprive the righteous of justice. ⁶A fool's lips walk into a fight, and his mouth invites a beating. ⁷A fool's mouth is his ruin, and his lips are a snare to his soul. ⁸The words of a whisperer are like delicious morsels; they go down into the inner parts of the body. ⁹Whoever is slack in his work is a brother to him who destroys.

What insight does God give us about applying our hearts to understand what He is saying in Scripture?

Take a minute and ask the Lord how He wants you to apply this Scripture to your life going forward (and we'll go around the room)?

#49   Luke 2:45-52 (WEB)

When they didn't find him, they returned to Jerusalem, looking for him. ⁴⁶ After three days they found him in the temple, sitting in the middle of the teachers, both listening to them, and asking them questions. ⁴⁷ All who heard him were amazed at his understanding and his answers. ⁴⁸ When they saw him, they were astonished, and his mother said to him, "Son, why have you treated us this way? Behold, your father and I were anxiously looking for you." ⁴⁹ He said to them, "Why were you looking for me? Didn't you know that I must be in my Father's house?" ⁵⁰ They didn't understand the saying which he spoke to them. ⁵¹ And he went down with them, and came to Nazareth. He was subject to them, and his mother kept all these sayings in her heart. ⁵² And Jesus increased in wisdom and stature, and in favor with God and men.

What insight does God give us about applying our hearts to understand what He is saying in Scripture?

Take a minute and ask the Lord how He wants you to apply this Scripture to your life going forward (and we'll go around the room)?

Appendix A – Instructor Guide for Interactive Bible Learning

A well-prepared Interactive Bible Learning (IBL) leader takes time to read and reflect on the questions before the meeting, documenting their own answers—not to "teach," but to create a more engaging and personal learning experience for everyone else.

The questions are designed to keep the group focused on the Bible passage being studied. Please try to avoid straying into unrelated philosophies, personal doctrines, or theological debates. This is more about *them* self-discovering a relationship with God through the Word of God (hear the Word). It's about *them* learning how to get understanding from the Holy Spirit who gives understanding; they will need His help to answer the questions. It's about *them* learning how to be doers of the Word. Your job is to keep the meeting focused on the Word. A well-run meeting is highly interactive, gentle, and full of love/truth. You will likely sense the presence and affirmation of the Holy Spirit, because the focus is on the Word, and the power is in the Word. And it should be fun learning together and watching one another grow.

Now, this may be hard for some, but leaders should resist the urge to *teach*. Instead, let it be about *them* learning. Let *them* process verbally; give *them* time to respond to the questions. If there are moments of silence, embrace them—it often means people are thinking, reflecting, or seeking the Holy Spirit's guidance. The goal is for *them* to self-discover the joy of reading, understanding, and doing the Word. This builds confidence in Christ. This lays a sure foundation which is the Word of God. And God does the increase.

Be more like an orchestra leader: keep the meeting moving along, keep it interactive, prefer others to self, and let them teach while you lead. One way to keep the meeting well balanced is to smile a lot, affirm responses, say "thank you" to show appreciation and love. If the conversation is going astray, repeat the question. Before moving onto the next question, always ask if anyone else has any thoughts about the question. Be encouraging, be gentle, be loving. Be patient with yourself and others throughout the learning process. Stay humble—sometimes you'll be teaching/leading, other times you will be learning/leading. Also, be aware that sometimes God anoints the least expected in the group to impact the life of someone else in the group, even better than you! That's not just okay—it's exciting. And God gets the glory!

The following is a typical meeting format...

1. **Open with Prayer**
   Begin the meeting with a prayer, inviting the Holy Spirit to lead the discussion and bring understanding.

2. **Ask someone to read**
   The facilitator invites a volunteer to read the Scripture passage aloud. This practice helps the group engage in both hearing and absorbing the Word.

3. **Read the first question**
   The leader reads the question first question, *"What insight does God give us in this Scripture about the topic we are studying?"*

4. **Orchestrate**
   The leader's job is to make sure everyone else is talking, interactive, learning, processing, edifying, building up, equipping, sharing. When someone is finished, thank them, ask if there is anyone else? Re-read the question if it's too silent or needs to be re-focused.

5. **Read the second question**

The second question (in case someone asks) is a question to help us know our enemy, which are distractions of the flesh, sin, world, and devil that keep us from hearing the Word and doing it.

6. **Read the last question**

   The last question is, *"Take a minute and ask the Lord how He wants you to apply this Scripture to your life going forward (and we'll go around the room)?"* After you read the question let the room be silent for a minute. It's a challenging question, but so important. Help them learn how to not only read the Word but do it (builds house on the rock). Then go around the room and make sure everyone shares. If they're not sure how to answer it, the first two questions will help them answer. No one is hidden.

7. **Close in Prayer**

   End the session with prayer. You may ask for prayer requests.

We suggest you commit to praying for one another throughout the study too.

Appendix B – The Good News

Jesus Christ is God's only Son, sent from heaven as the promised Messiah. Known as the Lamb of God and "Immanuel" (meaning "God with us"), He is the eternal Word who existed with God from the beginning and was sent to live amongst us. He was the only perfectly sinless person ever, coming from heaven to be the perfect sacrifice for our sins and unbelief. Jesus paid the ultimate price by shedding His blood on the cross—a necessary act for forgiveness, as God designed salvation to come through sacrifice. He willingly took our sines upon Himself. Jesus also rose from the dead, demonstrating His power over sin and death. He declared Himself that He is the resurrection and the life for all who believe. Through His sacrifice, Jesus reconciles us to God, grants us remission of sin and eternal life—a free gift given out of God's grace, mercy, forgiveness, and unfailing love. This is the Good News.

The Prayer of Faith

Our role is to believe and accept God's invitation for forgiveness and eternal life. We turn away from sin, repent of our past, and wholeheartedly trust Jesus—believing He is exactly who He claims to be and that His sacrifice is complete. By confessing Jesus as Lord over our lives, we receive forgiveness and the gift of the Holy Spirit—a gracious present from the Father, not something earned by our own effort.

Perhaps you already know these truths through your upbringing or by reciting the Apostles' Creed. Now, it's time to embrace them in your heart: Are you ready to leave your old life behind and follow Him? Are you prepared to accept the gift of new life in Christ? Do you want to be cleansed of all your sins? Are you willing to receive the glorious gift of the Holy Spirit to dwell within and guide you? Do you feel God drawing you closer to Himself?

If so, let's confess our faith in Jesus together. Please repeat after me:

"Jesus, I believe You are Immanuel—God with us. I believe You came from Heaven, died on the cross for my sins, and rose from the dead. I need a Savior, and that Savior is You, Jesus. I confess that I have sinned and fallen short. I turn to You now, leaving my old life behind. Please cleanse me of my sins and all unrighteousness."

[Pause to receive the forgiveness of sins.]

"Thank You for what You accomplished on the cross, for granting me eternal life, and for the gift of the Holy Spirit. I now receive Your Holy Spirit in my heart, in the name of Jesus."

[Pause again—allow time for the Holy Spirit to fill you. If appropriate, this may also be a moment for the laying on of hands in prayer.]

Now, let's take a moment to celebrate what the Lord has done! This is the beginning of a new life in Christ—one filled with His love, guidance, and constant presence. Welcome to the family of God!

www.ingramcontent.com/pod-product-compliance
Lightning Source LLC
Chambersburg PA
CBHW060408050426
42449CB00009B/1933